MOMENTS

This publication in the most loving memory of "Granny" Anne Teachworth.

Copyright © 2016 by jennskies

All rights reserved. This book or any portion thereof may not be reproduced or used in any manner whatsoever without the express written permission of the pub-lisher except for the use of brief quotations in a book review or scholarly journal.

First Printing: 2016
ISBN-10:0-9968648-2-4
ISBN-13:978-0-9968648-2-4

Jennifer Teachworth
PORTLAND, OR 97201

www.jenniferteachworth.com

Ordering Information:

Special discounts are available on quantity purchases by corporations, associa-tions, educators, and others. For details, contact the publisher at the above listed address. U.S. trade bookstores and wholesalers: Please contact Jennifer Teachworth jenn@jenniferteachworth.com

MOMENTS

Jennifer Teachworth

2016

for

jack + diane + john

&

joshua michael

OUTNUMBERED

"at least one of us is alive   if this is happening

either you are reading   or I am   statistics favor

you   it seems unfair   you get the living hands or I

will object   and kill you   not because I dislike you

because I like my life   and later today   in the

park   I will only apologize for my lack of regret   I

will eat grapes   I will lie on the grass   I will

have created a little impossibility   that's all I need

a way in   and then to unfold

like a bat"

- **HEATHER CHRISTLE**   *The Trees, The Trees*

TABLE OF CONTENTS

PROLOGUE // 11

BOOK ∞ I //
IT'S RARELY ONLY BLACK OR WHITE. // 15
I NEEDED PAIN TO KNOW LIFE. // 17
I FEEL SO NAKED RIGHT NOW. // 19
ON BUS, I FOUND MY SELF. // 21

BOOK ∞ II //
TAKE ME TO MY LAUGHING PLACE. // 25
KNEELING NEVER MADE SENSE TO ME. // 27
REMEMBER TO YELL
"HELP!" BEFORE DROWNING. // 29
PANIC PLAYED ME LIKE A FOOL. // 31
LETTING SIRI MISGUIDE ME THROUGH LIFE. // 33
TO THINK IS TO BE THOUGHTFUL. // 35
I DIDN'T WAIT FOR MARRIAGE REFORM. // 37

BOOK ∞ III //
NOTE TO SELF: MAKE MORE MONEY! // 41
I READ TOO MUCH EMILY DICKINSON. // 43
DO YOU NEED ROOM FOR CREAM? // 45
HURT CANNOT COME FROM YOU ANYMORE. // 49

EPILOGUE // 51

PROLOGUE

Each moment is one that takes you and grabs you, its title a memoir of your life in only six brief words.

Floating lightheadedness takes over your physical body—again. It has an effect where visual cues have dullness in color, a way of mentally hazing the reality your eyes show. Feet planted but entire body swaying until a hand—you realize it is your hand—catches the cool cement wall and ears start recognizing audible vibrations again.

That feeling there, even before you can really acclimate to your surroundings, that feeling keeps you hanging. It's a feeling like you've left home without your keys—every day of your life. The feeling of your ego dissipating, like that time Eric took LSD and called Maria because he thought the world had forgotten him. So you enter a crowd and this makes you feel even more alone.

this moment   brings knowledge   not afraid anymore
this moment   brings belief   landing feet   mark
the move   where you   lonesome   become you
courageous   heart is racing   unknown corridors
self wrapped heart's chambers   and corridors   some
dark   some listed   only on antiqued maps

BOOK ∞ I

IT'S RARELY ONLY BLACK OR WHITE.

how long until you're cured?   when will you have a life   you can afford?   aren't you tired   coming short?   haven't we been   over this   before?   it's unknown   what carries anxiety   lacking answers   to   formulaic inquisitions   not propriety   lacking answers   therapists   scientists   theologians   combined   cannot calculate   it has nothing to do with me   some embodiment   recalcitrant   it's not really so black or white and   for years   it's not been out of spite still   you dismiss this narrative as   contrived   trite   **There's no need for crying, get up and fight!**   but coin theories won't serve us well   more along a spectrum   still taking note of where   on it we fell   there's no end for winning   nor for a permanent Hell   every internal shift   self-propelled   not some result of faraway spells   answer to "Depressed?"   is **yes**   does it mandate a **no**   to "Happiness?"   it's not so black or white   it's really always a mess   the hue   determined   what we will to confess   it's rarely been so black or white   everything's more gray   in the light   in order to really know anything   we must accept   we know nothing   where has loss occurred   leaving   no discernible trace?   there's a hole there   in Its former place   no matter how bright my eyes   gray surrounds   our faces   getting worse   (just to get better)   requires   a certain   sort of   ***grace***

I NEEDED PAIN TO KNOW LIFE.

a fence that was not picket or white   a fence that was not actually there to stop Tyranny or its Fight from seizing any sense of self with just a stare   dedication to perfection was eradicated by fear: the all-purpose tool used since youth   (age three years in a place called Catholic school)   those formulas, scarlet letters, Awakenings, the Lord and history and its bias   stirred an inner turmoil   channeled into   physical conditionings   (one center of consistence)   even when patriarchal lessons   proven pointless   provided painful projections   love still lent appearances even among conditions   burdened by admonishing abuses   rather than disciplinary dysfunctions   then loud nights forced extroversion and
    copious cocktails   cigarettes   consumption of many sorts   the insignificant chatter of   gaudy people   found bland   enough for me   to forego expending energy on any sarcastic retorts   perhaps I am unfair   maybe   but my mind   too chaotic to care   I see lines of people boozing   contributing   evolutionary theories   of   hunched backs and crowed necks   coming soon in a   Darwinian future dirty dollars   liquor wells   glassy eyes   a yearning feeling   a serious complication   an inclination for urination
then   a fence that was not picket or white   a fence that was replaced with terrain   of thousands of miles some grit   some spite   schoolgirl of own domain   a future as a lady   a future of   love   a woman rising above   I was a girl who wrote my own acts of contrition   with long bouts of malnutrition   I am a woman who survived self-fumigation   misogynistic degradation   gained the strength   for construction of a fence   protected the production   of a site   that was an expression of my fight

I FEEL SO NAKED RIGHT NOW.

unpack emotional baggage   to really travel into the light   put its weight on the table   and step into the whirring world   with nothing on your person   but your self   bringing my worn-out tone of self condescension in ultimatums to no one but my self   speak today or forever deny all mental peace   but my words have always been   leading to this   well-kept notations of my many allusions   she's never been even a tad remiss chains keeping my silence   I put them on with my own hands   but their locks disintegrate   when in such empathic lands   my feet forget their freedom   lose their feeling   "I'm actually letting you see me like this!"   it helped me get to a place with a view   where vulnerability can be relative to bliss   the vulnerable soul: it soars and may nearly drown—but at least it moves   a celebration of tragedy makes many sounds   such conflictions of complexity   it still proves   living demands more   than going through motions   like going off the course   where the soul hides its truest devotions   takes an honest account of priorities   and of their order

ON BUS, I FOUND MY SELF.

my right leg   beneath me   bent at the knee   my eyes   gaze over lanes   my head   bobbing   I am just another girl   on the bus   looking expectantly   expecting an outcry   a passerby   some sighting of   my   failures   or   privileged pains   bare caution   before admitting defeat   try an   act   become   spectacle   boldly interrupt the   audible world's   humming   and   buzzing   and   stepping   and   shrieking too busy to   notice me   the bus bumps   unsettled souls shout   focused concern   my thoughts   deeper than   skin   beneath bone   burying below   future fractures   their spurs   impinged pain   accelerating self doubts   I gaze   beyond the window   the one (like all of them) with   smears showing   condensation   weather's bloodshed   from battling temperatures   with   every neighborly breath   someone takes   I   look at   my skin   its shade is fairness always fair? (no)   heard   an angry   shout   someone shoved   to the margins where though I am too   my margin mustn't   be   obvious enough   so push me there   with just   a stare because of my fine   and light brown   hair   I feel like I'm stealing another's air   see struggle   see it in   split hairs   under beanies   sweaty rain drizzled   on overcoats   maybe Johari manufactures bus windows   because   self-realizations rarely come   when   only with   your   self

BOOK ∞ II

TAKE ME TO MY LAUGHING PLACE.

doom as epic   doom as natural   a disaster. doom as female by name   but demon of demise   she was full   dirty water   took over home   so   when home was no more   safety   security   were   no more. dirty water stained   a new horizon   gained   family an apartment where   before   furniture had been living   alone but now   crying   on the couch   is a robe with a mother inside   a robe   with a mother inside   a suitcase with clothes for a daughter   outside   a hero hiding behind   a father   with tears   on a tarmac because   a daughter   with fears   a castle   gargoyles   a great place   my hand offered to shake an introduction   "come on, we can give hugs here," said mister kent jones   my heart   warming   I found a best friend   with tickling grins   chuckles turning upward a place with space for laughing   and where fears ought not deter   from authentic self's   crafting best friend Brynn let me in   took me down the hall   to space   where a yearbook letter   her to me   cover to cover   she let me know   I was the best at something   take me to my laughing place

KNEELING NEVER MADE SENSE TO ME.

it wasn't the Wednesday after Mardi Gras   but my soul fell   like ashes to the ground   in three languages, I can "Hail Mary"   with the Bible shut   words lacking belief still ringing   such familiar sounds   born and bred and educated and fed   on the command of the Pope   Catholic marks   I feel them   stinging my skull   through my forehead   a liturgical symphony of fear—silent sermons serving judgment   without my consent   "Catholic guilt," I've heard it called   my soul   the one that Dogma mauled   yet, I still cherish the discipline   (it's likely all I can believe in)   Mother Mary, it must have been so hard   "When did you stop believing in God?"   as if it were reductive   or something so   finite   if I had simply stopped believing, would it still keep me up at night? questioning my self-worth, feeling the tension stinging   my measurements   calculated through Doctrine   I never was one   to fit in   with those exclusivist   types

REMEMBER TO YELL "HELP!" BEFORE DROWNING.

a funny thing is the memory   of the who and of
the why   and of these the humor lies   in my
chosen avoidance   they barge in during my sleep,
contaminating my dreams like that fallen fly in the mason
jar   (half-full of wine, on my nightstand)   *dream*
can feel like flying blissfully   through an illuminated
night sky   just like "Peter Pan"   unless you're
more like me where   you're "funny" in memory
and   *dream*   just feels like a sewer dwelling
or like those scraps of trash   clogging gutter grates
flooding   of memories where death of the self   is
wholesale   every single night   another flood to
forge forward through

when it was just me and the flood   I was without a
boat   without an oar   I couldn't make peace with
the tide   I found the giving tree   an oar within
reach for when the tide gets high   and we have
ventured out to sea   we shake some of the weight
when these terrors of floods   like dreams flow
old skies can illuminate   and I can stand up   and walk
away

PANIC PLAYED ME LIKE A FOOL.

a jolt just above my rib cage   where a freeway of emotions merges in my chest   it's a blunt-force blow, powered with cloaked rage   like a foot stomping out breath   like mimicking cardiac arrest.   rib cage network collapses,   lethargy bottles up the conflicting emotions.   their conflicts?   the weight of Panic's rage (perhaps).   too major a network jam to move through   without mental confusion   sense of delusion   a visceral freeway   built   upon inner truths and then Panic blankets, making clear Her objectives.

   my self, silently crying out an SOS! to therapist, my emotional sleuth   she holds most qualified perspectives   for this high stakes pursuit.   even an emotional freeway emergency shoulder   gets jammed up (especially with its automatic transmission on a loop paved with irrational insecurities lacking enough awareness to find a way out that's not already fucked) automatic and repeating   bumper to bumper—thoughts getting stuck   Panic's hands rarely release her grip: your heart is her clutch.   emotions racing each other   trying to be seen in first place   all I feel is numb like needing my mother   instead, an orange bottle   holds my hand and strokes my face   orange bottles carrying first   responders: prescribed to sedate entire networks of   emotional freeways so neurons firing no longer have their previous priorities   a cocoon of yellow caution tape   I sigh   send everyone home   the evening's caput   on Tuesday   a thorough incident report to all my authorities   if safety is supposed to make me feel better, why does each ingestion go down like defeat?   like embodiment as perpetual debtor day after day   another Panic Jam   stuck on repeat.   though   I do enjoy the calm   from safely behind these closed and caution-taped frames   space   mental wandering   easier to find   when first responders play in Panic's game

belittled   that little white pill and then Panic melts;
              she becomes her former self

LETTING SIRI MISGUIDE ME THROUGH LIFE.

      all those memoirs telling of success after sins—
their briefest sections   those where recovery wins
heavy is their focus on maladjustment   moment after
moment   where Disorder is triumphant
  why? the authors lived long enough to tell? maybe it's
their way of exposing   intimate unmentionables
      without taking off a single garment.
all those words, printed on those papers   society's
discarded recyclables   shifting shame   selling
unrealistic   ideals   calling them works of art
it's the Getting Better Part   why I ingest every word
 "maybe this one will show me where to start" although,
instead, by the end, recovery only seems more absurd
if Recovery is about the   present moment   then why
do the plots   live   in the past?   specialists
spout Future is Important then predict one as a future
 lapsing acts   pinnacle of greatest battle
snuck in the back   just a quick caveat for an ending.
it is quite harder to think   nothing   of your self
and still fight for your   recovered existence   to
      prevail
than to think   nothing of your self and
    let your life and your mind be run by a scale
write moments of choice: the realizations to make a
decision and   right moments to use my voice
    toleration of discomfort a new acquisition
      but by now it's got to be said
it isn't a choice, not for lifestyle, not even partially. it's not
      the weight that really keeps me down
    Shame comes in a wrapper so dense,
the experience "deserves" more suffering than just its
proper noun *"it's just that Starving can make me less tense"*
I'm not here to defend Disorder and not here to detail
my Denials and I'm still here even without my own scale
on which to stand. there's not glory in my own death nor
    is it hiding in the spaces between my ribs

my fear of night may still cause unrest—
but now I wake up wanting to live   because
moment after moment   empty plate after empty plate
it's quantifiably less dishes to wash   and more hair to
pull out the drain

TO THINK IS TO BE THOUGHTFUL.

I sit below these trees   thinking thoughts to find logic in life and in its fees. I ration some money and I ration some reason.   I thought up a trail near Godot's last stop when Thinking thought, "perhaps I should fail, perhaps I ought not" sitting below these trees   imposing logical thinking upon dimensions clearly irrational   I'm drifting into the existential   my life's meaning   I lived to find—I lived and I died over and over   in my mind   then your kiss   a soul so kind

to think is
to be thoughtful   like the trail by the trees   like the virtue of the humble

to know thyself
is to have thought things through   to think when other would stagnate;   to be me—even with you.

I DIDN'T WAIT FOR MARRIAGE REFORM.

I didn't wait for marriage reform to tell me "it's okay to date" then I told my mother   she stared at the air like   it was full   toppling over Thanksgiving plates

it's kind of funny   when starting college and no one, not really even admission's officers   is recognizing real life knowledge   but it's okay—the most important truths I learned two doors down where my former friendships   my former self   all were far away then my acceptance   being gay   but what's with the need for labels anyway?   strong, thoughtful—it's your voice that I hear   voice so pure   honest— but that's not what makes me queer   a voice   a vision   everyone needs to hear   everyone needs to see   *because art moves people*   *who are standing still*   before I met you   I was dead   as I was ill

BOOK ∞ III

NOTE TO SELF: MAKE MORE MONEY!

a post-it on my desk   or in a drawer   or in a bin—somewhere
a note on a post-it that was written years ago   where the minimum wage   all we can expect to get paid   is like the second model of an 8-track player   in a world where thousands of tracks   can weightlessly exist on a wrist

a conundrum coined classic   "act like an adult!" so to myself but from someone else I wrote: "make more money, this is your note!"   money as a meter of self-worth (not just net-worth)   lose self   get caught in the net   have you heard that for tomorrow we are left without guarantee?   for my always wanting endless days with you   penny over penny I'd borrow but to make more money just a little   just enough so that if tomorrow's sunset   were to take me with it a room to yourself you could have   with a place to sit   it could be nice to   cosmically buy you a drink and maybe for a spell   it could make the whole of my absence shrink   because even when meant well a note to self   to make more money   is entirely worthless, honey

what I'll always make (even if push didn't come to shove) is more time with you, m'love

I READ TOO MUCH EMILY DICKINSON.

I remember what I've lost like when I lost my will for life
            (or for most things innate to it)
I remember my voice   how it no longer made actual
sound   but still spoke loud "truths"   within my
mind   I remember my surrender and humiliation
my naïveté;   his objectification   his foul play

in many mornings after my surrender   I may as well
have had my head in an Emily Dickinson book
reading all the ways I could express   such distaste
of feeling him   still stuck   in my gut

but instead, I drifted my   descent down   curved
stairs   to my father in the kitchen I held out to him my
  bowl, full with milked cereal: *"Dad! I no longer like milk.
  It has become another thing I suddenly cannot stand!"*
   my parents, why had they not asked me why I had gone
away?   instead they thought their daughter
    missing, "Just put her face on milk carton boxes, old
school style"   why did they not try another way?
       what if someone had just asked,   *are you okay?*
moments of remembering my surrendering   eliminates
essential   life-affirming abilities   like remember-
ing self-worth   how my voice can carry my self   or
what   existence   felt like   before   it felt like this:
   like always breathing underwater when I remember my
first   I don't get nostalgic   or sentimental. I
get panic   and I get accidental
self-conscious   emotionally avoidant   I thought
I had no value because   he had taken it
all by force   instead of walking away   I spent years still
dragging along   that cobbled rock road every
backwards and sideways direction.   when I remem-
ber then   I remember what living was like: sleeping
with dread   waking up with a soul so dead.
   I remember the rocks and the threats—I remember the

dark-watered ditch   because when I remember
my *First*   I have to remember   him   angry and
statutory   I have to remember   me   afraid at
                        age thirteen
I remembered that *First*   but then I remembered my
love this morning   I felt her arms   wrap   all the
way around me   for this moment it is love I hold on to

DO YOU NEED ROOM FOR CREAM?

a mish-mash of a schedule with a first alarm around last call at the bars   punching the four AM clock can be dreadful   my car-share route to work lit by stars.   the risks for oversleeping: a barista befallen exhaustion   a phone left on silent   rivals those other thrills and risks that   would make this job impossible for keeping

"you are far too brilliant," (my father admits), "to be pouring people's coffees!"   then I've lost him again   defense is rarely a preferred strategy in a battle without exits   so no more of my saying   words together proving this isn't   my destination

this café as an ornamental *Third Place*   where even the green straws have a standard   and regulars frequent just to see another familiar face   an expedited drink order only adds to the glamour

whether it's a caffeine withdrawal migraine on the mind or their cabstand is without a line   I meet the greatest diversity of people who are kind   and   in no other setting would our conversations align

they come with such adoration   blessing us for our refusal to submit   to Mr. Sandman's bags of optical abrasion—as though for our sleep he arrives with a writ. not every barista shares my same intentions. despite the corporate assumption   working downtown requires certain gumption.

our common ground is in the beans between the conversations   creating another's experience through means in our existence with   the smallest insight spawning revelations

maybe through talking to people who are standing idly

by,   I'm able to actually learn   a little more deeply
the true agonies of those who need support; like understanding humanity through building rapport
those lessons are irrevocably life sustaining
the permanence of such life wisdom adds to my hourly gaining
maybe my decision   to really study the human condition   instead of a fast-tracked MBA
from an accredited institution is because   I find value   where others may find   only spite and that I can write my hindsight.   it's not that I'm without my own bitterness benders   where my outlook goes askew;   I fear I'll turn into one of those   pretenders   where nothing of my self is true. my college terms turned seasonal breaks   brought my independent study to the startling discovery   of authentic wisdom   in regular people with regular takes
      who've leant unspoken support aiding in my recovery.   the favorites whose drinks I've perfected have taught me the possibility of acceptance   because they heard me and still connected   (even when I felt paralyzed with reluctance).   it was opening up to strangers and letting them connect with me
that I felt heard   in real time   speaking truths more timeless than any virtual platform   could ever allow.
these are the thoughts that span a route to work that is lit by stars—for now.

HURT CANNOT COME FROM YOU ANYMORE.

there's a part   on our bodies   just above our hearts   on paper   I write your name   that part of my body   just above   my heart   aches there's a part   on our bodies   the one that   makes us tremble   at work   I write   your name   that part of my body   within my hands   unsteady   there's a part of our bodies   in neural networks   like   memories in our brains   in memories   I write   your name   that part of my body   somewhere in my brain   comatose   there's a part of our bodies   just within all of us   our souls   in sleep   I write   your name   that part of my body   my soul   the only part of me   you couldn't steal

 heart aches   +   hands tremble + brain comatose = my soul   sighs   there goes another afternoon

EPILOGUE

a moment of clarity starts to end
the pangs of humiliation return with a greater frequency
and volume (like right now)
now is when my breath is getting more shallow but
I'm doing all the moves I know to keep it as deep as
possible
I start to go away and
usually I would hit cancel
twice
but I'm going to hit send
instead
I'm going to try to stay present
talking to you via this blank composition
because I don't want to go away right now
don't want to make myself feel humiliated or
disconnected
only so this spectacle called
"life: the inner narrative"
will go on
I want to be able to skip that step;
that step is so maladaptive—it physically hurts

I want to just stay here talking to you
and remembering that in this street fight:
the opponents have a lot of masks,
and sometimes they look like our own selves.

ACKNOWLEDGMENTS

...the strongest people I know who have generously provided me with their time to listen to me, their advice to my confused stares, their strength in allowing me to be vulnerable in front of them, their voice and electronic mail boxes for my middle of the night letters...

I am incredibly grateful to still have my life with a beating heart and thoughtful mind. Thank you for giving me my life back, one way or another—through the safety you have created for me or the friendship you have honored me with maintaining.

Maria, my wife partner, for always sharing the weight of the world with me.

Whitney, my big sister, for giving me little sister survival skills.

Emma Willard School, for saving my life through education.

Mr. Lucky & Lucille Simone for always providing me with unspoken emotional support.

My many friends whom always love me, despite (or because of) my eccentricites—

Thank you to everyone who offered support during the revealing process—I have loved you all so very much and I am eternally grateful for the confidence you have helped me build.

www.ingramcontent.com/pod-product-compliance
Lightning Source LLC
LaVergne TN
LVHW091320080426
835510LV00007B/576